LUCKY:

The Squirrel With A Tale

by TK Harmon

Trafford PUBLISHING® www.trafford.com

North America & international
toll-free: 1 888 232 4444 (USA & Canada)
phone: 250 383 6864 ♦ fax: 812 355 4082

DEDICATIONS

First and foremost, this book is dedicated to GOD as the Creator of the Universe – thank you, Lord, for all the wonderful creatures in it.

Secondly, to my Mom and Dad as the Creators of *my* world – thank you both for instilling in me a love for all God's creatures.

Last, but certainly not least, thanks to Lucky for allowing me to be a part of her life, if even for a short time…

A special thanks to **Shylo Spears** for the time spent on the beautiful illustrations.

CONTENTS

Chapter 1

LUCKY'S BEGINNING

The time had come to let her go, and it was going to be hard on me. As much as I disliked the idea, she deserved to be among her own kind to find a mate and have a family. She had only been a part of my life for a short time, but it had been extraordinary, and I would truly miss her. I couldn't help worry about her and could only pray that God would keep her safe, this funny little creature that had taught me so much.

As my friend and I nailed her nesting box high in a tree, preparing to release her, my mind raced over her antics of the past eleven months, from that very first day with me . . .

We lived in a small town at the edge of a national forest; so naturally, we saw a lot of wildlife. I fed the squirrels, birds, chipmunks—just about anything that wandered by wanting food. One afternoon, I was at the kitchen sink, looking out in the backyard. I was watching two of my cats sitting at ninety-degree angles from a hollyhock that had sprung up in my lawn. They weren't moving, and I became curious. I figured they were watching a bug or an earthworm. Several minutes later, I decided to check it out.

Under that hollyhock was the tiniest creature I'd ever seen. It was so small that I thought it was a baby chipmunk. I quickly pushed the cats and dogs into the house, figuring the little animal would run away after they were gone. But when I returned, it was still there. I thought it might be hurt, so I started talking very softly. The baby didn't move—it only stayed in one position, watching me. I knelt to see if it was hurt. It didn't run away; it just sat blinking at me, breathing rapidly. Upon closer examination, I realized it wasn't a chipmunk at all, but a tiny rock squirrel. I talked to it softly for ten or fifteen minutes. I told the little squirrel it was really lucky to have escaped my pets and that it ended up with someone wanting to help.

"That's it! I'll call you 'Lucky,' since that could be either a girl's or a boy's name, even though I am referring to you as 'him.'" Then, I placed my hand, palm up, on the sidewalk, figuring the movement might cause Lucky to run away; but if it didn't, then I would decide what to do next. The baby immediately ran to me, sniffed each finger, and proceeded to climb up.

I almost yelped in surprise. Standing up slowly, holding the squirrel, I stroked his head a few times. Lucky, lying on his tummy, stretched out in my hand. His back feet barely stuck over the tips of my fingers, and the front feet, which I thought of as "hands," almost reached the bend at my wrist. I examined Lucky more closely and noticed that his ears weren't fully opened. He *was* young. I also noticed the poor thing was covered with fleas and lice or mites, which were crawling on my hand and hopping onto my white shirt. Not knowing how long Lucky had been here, I figured he must be hungry and thirsty. I sat him down under the hollyhock and went to find him food and water.

The adult squirrels eat the birds' seed, so I placed a small amount in the lid of a jar and some water in another lid. When I put them on the sidewalk, Lucky scurried over, stuck his head down as though to drink, ended up sticking half his face in the water, and pulled back, shocked. The seed held absolutely no appeal. *Being so small,* I thought, *maybe he needs milk.* He was really young, so I knew he needed more than the two percent milk that I drank. I grabbed some canned milk, mixed it with water, and added a drop of honey. But the same thing happened. *The poor thing doesn't know how to drink,* I thought. He was probably not yet weaned from mama's milk, since he was so small.

The whole time I was trying to figure out how to feed this animal, I was also wondering how it got in my backyard. There were no holes in the ground, and he was too tiny to have made it all the way to the hollyhock with the cats and dogs outside. The only possibility I could think of was that a large bird might have picked him up for a snack and then dropped him in the yard. The crows were always bringing "creatures" to wash in the birdbath, so that was a real possibility.

I remembered an old eyedropper in the bathroom that might help in feeding him. I sterilized it with boiling water, filled it with the milk mixture, and headed back to the baby. Lucky was still under the hollyhock but came running when I bent down with my outstretched hand. He climbed up, and, when I offered him the eyedropper, he grabbed it with his tiny hands and drank. Then he didn't want me to take it away to refill it. I had to pry it away from him, and we went through this three more times. When he was finally full, he turned his head away, stretched out in my hand, and went to sleep in the warm sunshine, which was now causing sweat to form a little river down my back.

I stood a little while longer trying to figure out what to do with him. I decided to put him under the lilac bush because that would offer him more protection from predators. I went to the closest pet store and purchased a small cage, figuring I could at least give him some place to grow in until he became big enough to have a fighting chance when released. When I got back, Lucky wasn't under the lilacs. After quickly looking around the area, I spied him standing in the doorway of the doghouse. I was thankful he'd made it back across the vast expanse of lawn with no apparent problems. After slowly walking over to the doghouse, I offered my hand, and again, he climbed in it. I had filled his cage with aspen shavings and put in a tissue box where he could nestle. I had also purchased a couple of toys that I thought might keep him occupied. He checked everything out and then disappeared into the box. Now, I knew how new moms felt . . . I fed that tiny creature with the eyedropper every four hours for the next two weeks. I went out during the night and woke him up. He sleepily drank his milk and crawled right back in his box.

The day after I found him, I called my veterinarian to see what I needed to be feeding Lucky. The vet recommended I bring Lucky in immediately so he could be flea-dipped and checked out; the Hanta Virus and the Plague were in our area. The vet told me he thought "he" was a "she," though he couldn't tell for sure. Then, Dr. Rick gave "her" a flea bath. Lucky didn't squirm much and actually seemed relieved; the bugs began falling off immediately. The vet dried her, combed her, and sent us on our way after giving me a few ideas for her food.

During the two-week eyedropper period, the nights were very cold, so I kept Lucky in the garage and put the cage in half sun/half shade during the day. I researched squirrels on the internet and learned a few things, though everything I read said squirrels were mean and, as such, needed to be handled with care.

Lucky grew quickly and became adventuresome. With each growth phase, I purchased a larger cage. I ended up with a six-foot ferret cage on wheels that I could easily move. Often, she ate, then ran up my arm to my shoulder, crossed over the back of my neck, ran down the other arm, and then jumped to her cage. As soon as I was ready to close the door, she'd spin around and startle me by jumping back onto my shirt or my shoulder and do the whole routine again. I bought her an exercise wheel, which she used regularly; but she still preferred my body as her workout center.

One day, after making a batch of Rice Krispie treats, I went out to see Lucky while I was eating one of them. She reached through the cage and grabbed a piece of the treat. Surprised to find that she wanted what I was eating, I opened the cage door and offered her another piece. Grabbing it away from me, she proceeded up my arm to eat her treat on my shoulder. She also liked to play with my hair, so I tried to get her off my shoulder because I didn't want her sticky "fingers" in my hair. At that point, she had finished her treat and reached over and took mine from me. I was so astonished that I just let her take it. When she was satisfied that there were no more treats coming, she calmly went back in her cage.

Over the next couple of months, I had a grand time with Lucky, while trying not to get too attached as I'd be releasing her soon. She was a wild animal and deserved to be free; I only wanted to let her get big enough to have a fighting chance. I knew the right time to let her go would present itself to me. In the meantime, I planned to enjoy this funny little squirrel that traveled with me, went to family reunions, chased my cats, and disliked men. But *those* are stories for another time.

Alert &
Hungry

One of us is a
little messy!

Eating is hard work!
It exhausts me

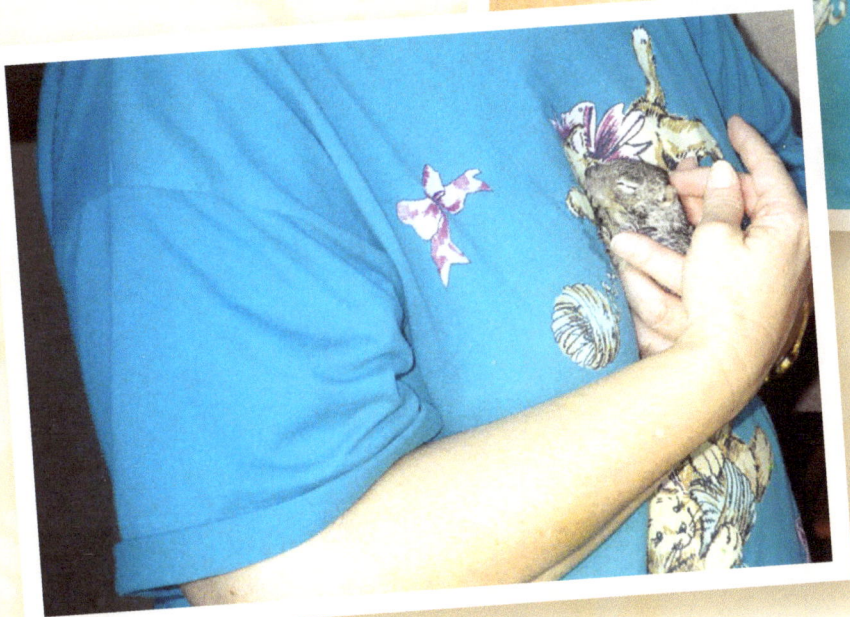

Chapter 2

LUCKY'S REIGN OF TERROR

As the little squirrel grew bigger on a *daily* basis, I constantly looked for things to do to keep her mind occupied. She was extremely curious, and I wanted to help develop her mind if I were going to keep her in captivity until she matured enough to release. I spent a great deal of time with her every day, between feedings and keeping her cage clean, so I was able to watch her enjoy the various toys I bought her.

After the first two weeks, Lucky began eating hard food on a regular basis. I tried sticking to items that she would find in the wild, but the snows had begun to cover the ground, which made walking through the forest difficult. So, the produce department of the local grocery store became my "forest" for Lucky's food. I tried all kinds of food on her. Some were obvious, and she really liked them, like the peanuts, pecans, and almonds that I left in the shells so she could exercise her jaws and teeth. Others were not so obvious, and I would have to try little bits at a time to see if she liked them. She enjoyed carrots, corn-on-the-cob, and apples, but definitely disliked pears, as well as alfalfa sprouts, cauliflower, and broccoli. I developed a friendship with our local grocer after he became curious as to why I wanted only four bean sprouts or one asparagus stalk. After explaining, the grocer not only wouldn't let me pay for my tiny samplings of fruits and vegetables, but he also began coming up with different things for me to try on the squirrel.

The tissue box I had originally put in the cage for her to sleep in was quickly demolished by her sharp teeth, and she thoroughly enjoyed tearing it up in little pieces. At first, I picked up the pieces and threw them away. Then, I put another empty box in, just to watch her run to it and start tearing it up as well. I finally let her keep the pieces to use in building her "nest," since she seemed so determined. I realized the box-demolishing was a game to her, but she left herself without a place to hide or to sleep away from the curious eyes of the household cats and dogs.

I bought her a "nesting box" for birds and placed it in the bottom of her cage. The cage had litter of aspen shavings and various grasses on the floor. I knew from watching that Lucky would carry what she wanted into her new "den" to make a cozy bed, so I provided ample "furnishings" to keep her occupied. But watching her trying to get *in* the nesting box through the small hole was a sight to behold. After stuffing the house with grasses, she tried to go through head first, but her body was too big. She was *not* going to let that deter her, however, and began trying to *pull* herself through the hole. Her little hind legs and big rump dangled outside the box as she tried, unsuccessfully, to wiggle her way through. My laughing, I believe, perturbed her greatly—at least judging by the look on her face. She was not happy that all her labor was for naught, and she disappeared up to another level of the cage where she began making her "clicking" noises at me. She made these noises whenever it appeared she was scolding me for something she didn't like.

I took the nesting box out, dumped the contents into a cardboard box, and proceeded to the garage, where I could use a saw to make the opening larger. I made it *quite* a bit larger so that, as she grew, she would be able to get through. A nesting box has a lid that is hinged so that it rises up with a slight push. After I put the contents back into her "house" and put the house back into the cage, Lucky immediately went through the opening and explored her new "digs." Satisfied with what she found, she then tried the lid, pushing it up to stick her head out. She looked at me as if to say, "This will do, for *now*!"

Since the snows had come and the garage was a stand-alone structure, I figured it got too cold at night for her. She was, after all, still a baby with little resistance; so, I brought the six-foot cage into my bedroom and placed it in front of the sliding glass door on a large piece of indoor/outdoor carpet for easy cleaning. Of *course* the cats had to check her out, so they hesitantly inched their way up to the cage. Lucky was sitting above their view, on her haunches, peering down at them curiously. When two of the cats put their paws on the cage to stretch up and get a closer look, instead of running to a higher level, Lucky charged them. Terrified, they scattered to the winds. I don't know what she would have done had they not moved, but luckily, we didn't have to find out.

After the cats got used to her being there and running on the exercise wheel at all hours, they pretty much ignored her—until she wanted a distraction. When that was the case, she would wait until they were walking past and then begin pummeling them with pecan or almond shells. She had tried it with peanut shells, but found they were too light to make it to her target. I couldn't believe it. She was actually playing with them like mean little school kids play dodge-ball.

One day, I had her on my shoulder while I was walking around the house. I had taken her into the kitchen for a Rice Krispie Treat, which she rarely got since I was sure the sugar wasn't good for her. She had enjoyed the walk, running from shoulder to shoulder to see what was around her. When I returned to my room to put her back in her cage, *she* decided she wasn't ready to go in yet. She proceeded to jump onto my bed, then down to the cedar chest, and then onto the floor. I quickly shut my door so she wouldn't venture out into the rest of the house where I might never catch her. She ran under the bed, which terrorized the cat in residence there. The cat hissed and ran to the other side of the room. Lucky found this most interesting and took off in hot pursuit. I couldn't help but burst out laughing, which scared Lucky, who ran under the bedside table. I began talking quietly, hoping to calm her. I eased the bottom drawer open, and she popped her head up like a Jack-in-the-Box. I laughed again, and she darted out of sight.

I couldn't figure out where she'd gone, until I opened the top drawer and up popped her head again. This went on for several minutes, first one drawer and then the other. She finally tired of this game and took off to the dresser, behind which were all kinds of electrical cords and wiring. I was concerned that she might get shocked if she bit into one of the wires, so I began coaxing her toward her cage. I had the cage door open, but she couldn't get in because it was too high, without any "hand" holds. While she explored my bedroom, and, consequently, chewed through the telephone wire, I engineered a ramp so she could get *herself* back into the cage, since she didn't want my help. Two hours later, she was tired and went peacefully into her cage. She crawled into her house, pushed the straw and grasses up in front of the opening as though for privacy,

curled up, and went to sleep. I could see enough of her to realize she was sleeping like one of the cats she so often watched, curled around with a paw over the eyes, nose tucked in. Okay, was Lucky having an identity crisis? Did I need to limit her exposure to the cats? What about the dogs? Well, I guessed I didn't have to worry about them. One had gotten too close to her, and she had scratched his nose through the cage. That's all it took. Word got out to the others, and they were steering clear of her! As far as they were concerned, the little terror had my room all to herself. In fact, they didn't even want to go when I visited my mom, since Lucky would be traveling with me. *Oh well,* I thought, *I guess it'll be just the squirrel and the "squirrely human" this trip.*

Chapter 3

LUCKY GOES TO "GRANDMA'S"

Lucky had me wrapped around her little finger, and I believe she was well aware of that fact. If she wanted something, she chirped at me, and the volume determined how quickly I responded. If one of the pets got too close, and she didn't have shells to throw at them, she would call me *loudly* to let me know she was bothered. I'd run into the room and make all the pets leave. Lucky was fine with my rapidity and would go on about her business, usually the business of cleaning house. She was definitely a "neatnik" extraordinaire.

Shortly after moving her into my room, I discovered she *hated men*! When any man went near her cage, she threw herself at the side, grabbing the bars with her little paws and rattling the cage while spitting and hissing at him. The scenario reminded me of a gorilla at the zoo who has gotten mad at people poking things in his cage. So I knew that when I went to my mom's, I'd have to take Lucky with me in order for her to get fed and to have fresh water and clean litter.

Breaking down her six-foot cage for transport, I put her in one of her smaller cages. I had already put a sheet over the back seat and arranged it so she wouldn't be in the hot sun for the whole trip. New toys were a necessity, as well.

Lucky absolutely *loved* toys designed for ferrets, especially those that rattled and were covered with sisal rope. In a matter of an hour, she frequently had the new toy reduced to a pile of rope that she began detangling so she could use the strands in her "house." The chewed up "thing" that the rope had covered was in a heap in the bottom of the cage. She didn't mind if I removed the "thing," but if I tried to remove

any of the rope, she grabbed it from the opposite end and started yanking on it. This, I gathered, was her way of saying, "Hands off! This is mine!" I tried gently pulling it away from her, but this began a game of tug-of-war. She was strong, but I was stronger. The first time I took the rope away from her, thinking she might choke on it, she looked so sad and hurt that I quickly stuck it back in the cage, which perked her right up. She grabbed the rope and rushed into her house with it. After that, I only removed the "thing" part of her toys, figuring she really didn't need to be swallowing plastic.

I was only going to my mother's for a few days, but, by taking Lucky with me, I ended up loading the car for what looked like a month's stay. Lucky made an enjoyable traveling companion. She busied herself cleaning house, chirping at me when I talked to her, playing with her toys, and sleeping. It was a four-hour trip, so I stopped at one of the rest stops to stretch my legs. Looking in the back seat, I realized Lucky had managed to get a hold of the sheet that I had draped over the seat; she had pulled it into the cage as far as she could. This had been a feat for her, since it was a king-size sheet, but she had pulled almost a quarter of it into the cage and had been sleeping on it. Once she could no longer pull anymore of it through the cage, she had begun yanking on it and succeeded in shredding the sheet into nice, convenient little pieces that she could manage. Oh well, thank goodness I no longer had a king-size bed!

The trip went off without a hitch, and when we arrived at Mom's, I quickly unloaded everything and put Lucky's six-foot cage together so I could get her into a larger, more comfortable space.

Mom hadn't met the squirrel yet, but when I took Lucky out of her small cage, she ran up my arm to my shoulder and sat looking at Mom as if to say, "OK, you're small. You don't pose any threat, so I guess I like you." I introduced the two of them, and Mom, never surprised at any animal I brought home, said, "I think I have some pecans and pine nuts in the freezer. We'll have to get them out for her." Yep, I could already see she was going to spoil Lucky.

As we stood talking, Lucky decided to venture out and explore . . . Mom's shoulder. When she jumped down to Mom's level, I had to peel the poor woman off the ceiling. I said, "Lucky, that wasn't a very nice thing to do to 'Grandma.' You scared her."

To which my mother replied, "Yes, you did! And if you scare me like that again, you'll end up as squirrel soup!"

Now, *I* knew she was kidding, but I don't think Lucky did. And, I truly believe Lucky understood her because she promptly jumped back up onto my shoulder and raced across my back to the other shoulder where she could peek around my head to see where Mom was standing. After that, whenever I'd take Lucky out of her cage and Mom was standing anywhere close, I'd warn her that Lucky might jump over to her shoulder, which she usually did. But Mom was ready for her and quit flinching when the squirrel jumped over to her shoulders and played in her hair. "Grandma" just took it in stride as she always did with the "critters" I brought home.

A gentleman neighbor came to visit, as he did on a daily basis to check on Mom. He was fascinated by the little squirrel, but Lucky *did not* like him . . . he was a man! He wanted her to jump from my shoulder to *his* shoulder like she did with mom, but Lucky would have no part of that. I protected her by putting her back into the cage where she felt safe, and she ran from floor to floor and dove into her nesting box.

Mom did clean all the nuts out of her freezer, and, when we left a week later, I had enough nuts for Lucky and half the squirrel population in the forest. They would last a long time because I only gave them to her a couple of times a week. I wanted her to have a well-balanced diet—at least as well balanced as I could figure out from the research I had done.

When we left Mom's house, she seemed sad to see Lucky go. She enjoyed watching the squirrel play, and she enjoyed it when Lucky used her arms as a racetrack, now that she was used to it. I assured her Lucky and I would be back soon. In fact, it would only be about three weeks before we were scheduled to pick Mom up to attend a large reunion. I would again have to bring Lucky along to ensure that she was taken care of and given food and fresh water. That meant she would be staying in the hotel with us, and I couldn't imagine what the housekeeping staff would think. But I couldn't worry about it now; Lucky *had* to attend the reunion.

I get to try nuts now!

Chapter 4

THE FAMILY REUNION

The family reunion was set for Labor Day, which meant three days in a motel in a small town. That would be three days of sharing a room with my mom and a squirrel—now, that would be interesting.

The days were too hot to take Lucky to the campsite where the family would be gathering. It would be much more comfortable for her if we left her at the motel in the air-conditioned room. Plus, I wouldn't worry about the number of people milling around her since she was quite a conversation starter. I took plenty of pictures with me to show everyone my new "baby" and those first days of feeding with the eyedropper, sitting on my shoulder eating Rice Krispie Treats, in various cages, etc. I had plenty of stories to tell the family about *my* family.

That weekend was spent in a whirlwind of activity—family events, playing with Lucky, and cleaning up after her. One afternoon, we got back to the room early, and the housekeeper was just finishing up her duties. She informed us, laughingly, that she had vacuumed our carpet three times. Each time she completed the chore and began wrapping the electrical cord around the vacuum, Lucky chirped at her as though to get her attention, then ran to the edge of the cage and kicked up the cedar shavings in such a way as to push them through the cage and onto the floor. Then, she ran up to the next level and chirped loudly as though she were saying, "Ha-ha-ha. You only *thought* you were through. Look, what a mess!" The housekeeper unwrapped the cord and plugged it in again, all the time scolding Lucky for making the mess. When she started up the vacuum, Lucky just sat on the upper level and waited for her to finish, then ran down and created another mess.

After the second time, the housekeeper had a clever idea. She got a couple of nuts from the supply bag we had left on the dresser, and as soon as she had finished vacuuming for the third time, but before Lucky could scurry down to the lower level, she pushed a couple of the nuts through the cage next to the squirrel. That occupied Lucky long enough for the housekeeper to finish with the vacuum and put it out of sight. She finished cleaning the room with no further antics from Lucky. Mom and I both grabbed our wallets to get some money for the housekeeper. She very sweetly said, "Oh, you don't need to do that."

"But she caused you added work. It's only fair. Look at what time it is. She probably put you behind schedule," I said.

"No, ma'am. It's okay, really. I actually look forward to this room. She's the most unusual pet I've ever seen come through here. And she's funny. She makes me laugh."

Needless to say, when we checked out of the room, we left the housekeeper a nice note with a large tip!

The last morning at the motel, I took Lucky's cage out to the lawn to clean it before we left. As I was going about my business, a little boy of about six or seven years old came over to ask what I was doing. I explained it to him as his mother joined us. I told the boy, "Make sure you don't put your fingers in the cage because she bites." His mother reiterated as she saw him get ready to stick his fingers through. Then, she gave him an ultimatum of bodily injury from the squirrel and loss of television-watching privileges if he didn't listen to her. What did he do? Of course, he stuck his fingers in, and Lucky bit him. Thankfully, he either didn't get his hand in very far, or Lucky was only warning him, because she didn't break the skin.

I was worried what the mother would say or do, but she only said, "Well, I *told* you to keep your fingers out of the cage. That's what you get for disobeying. Maybe next time, you'll listen to me!"

I quickly finished the clean-up process after that and grabbed our suitcases, Mom, and the squirrel. Then, I shoved everything into the car and headed out of that town before the woman could change her mind and possibly cause trouble.

I love Vegas in Spring!

Treats in Vegas

Treats in Vegas

If you don't give it to me, I'll just take yours!

My penthouse in Vegas

Chapter 5

LUCKY'S NARROW ESCAPE

When Lucky was about six months old, I thought she was ready to be released. Taking her up the hill from our house, I opened the cage door and coaxed her out onto my shoulder. I bent over so that she wouldn't have so far to jump; she leaped to the ground and scampered up a tree. I watched her for a few minutes as she explored the tree and surrounding area. Picking up the cage, I headed back to the house, turning around every so often to make sure she wasn't following me. I needn't have worried; she was too busy investigating her new surroundings. I was concerned about her all evening and didn't sleep well that night. Something just didn't seem right.

The next morning, I couldn't get it out of my head that something was wrong. I just had this feeling that I needed to go look for Lucky—now. I grabbed my jacket and a handful of almonds, and darted out the door. I began calling Lucky's name and then listening for her. Except for the twittering of the birds and the occasional buzzing of insects, there was no other sound. I felt a rising panic because I *knew* something was wrong; I could *feel* it. I explored all around our house, over hill and dale, and kept calling Lucky's name—nothing. Then, a terrible thought crept into my head. The day before, after I released her, I watched other squirrels playing on my neighbor's woodpile and wondered if Lucky would find them and become friends. I prayed that she didn't because my neighbor, Sam, trapped squirrels and shot them. Being an animal lover, I *hated* that idea, but Sam said they were too big of a nuisance and too destructive. His car ended up costing over $2,000.00 to repair because a squirrel chewed through the electrical wiring. I was curious how he knew it was a squirrel, as I was sure he hadn't actually *seen* a squirrel chewing it, and some other creature could have done it. We had field mice that could have done it or a gopher or mole, but I didn't ask Sam because he *really* disliked squirrels. The thought of him shooting squirrels, however, was enough to send me charging through the back pasture to his house.

I didn't really know Sam all that well; he was a bit of a loner. So, I approached his house cautiously. I called Lucky's name again and felt chills run up my spine as she answered me in a *shrill* scream. At first I wasn't sure it was her. I called her name again, and the same cry came back to me. As I sprinted the last hundred yards to his house, I continued calling her name, and she continued answering. When I got closer to his house, I felt my heart in my throat. There she was, trapped in one of his cages. When she saw me, she stuck her little arms through the cage and flexed small fingers in a gesture that reminded me of a small child waving for his mom to come to him. I rushed over to her and knelt by the cage, but I couldn't figure out how to open it! Panic again set in, and I knew I'd have to get Sam to open the cage. Not knowing how long she had been captured, I thought she might be hungry; I pushed a couple of almonds through the cage. But she was too afraid to think about eating, I guess, because she wouldn't take her eyes off me long enough to get the nuts. She kept grabbing for me, and, as I headed for Sam's house, Lucky uttered the strangest sound, as though she were pleading with me not to leave her.

When my relentless knocking got no response, I barged in through the unlocked door, yelling, "Sam, I want Lucky back!"

Sam came into his kitchen with a look of surprise as if to say, *What do you want? I don't recall asking you to come in, so why are you standing in my kitchen?* But he only asked, "What?"

"You have Lucky trapped in your cage, and I want her back," I said, still greatly bothered by the fact that he trapped squirrels and shot them. *How barbaric of him,* I thought.

"Oh, that's *your* squirrel? Well, it really is a lucky squirrel, because I was just getting ready to go shoot it." I could feel the blood drain from my cheeks at that thought. "Yeah, go ahead and take it, but you better let it go somewhere else, because if it comes back here, it'll just get trapped again; next time, it might not be so lucky."

I thought to myself, *you bet I will! But I know she's smarter than that. I bet she wouldn't get trapped by you again because she wouldn't take the chance on a jerk like you shooting her.* But what I actually said was, "Well, I'm really glad I listened to my heart and felt an urgency to come find her."

He showed me how to open the cage and told me to go ahead and borrow it to get her home. I took Lucky back to her cage in my room, and she seemed genuinely pleased to be back in a safe environment. She drank water for a long time and then began to eat the veggies and nuts I brought her.

I actually thought about not returning the trap to Sam. That way, he couldn't trap any more animals and shoot them while they were sitting in his cage, defenseless. But that wasn't honest, and I knew he had other cages, anyway; he was determined to shoot trapped squirrels!

It frightened me to think how close she had come to being a target for what I considered a lunatic. "Well, Lucky, looks like you'll be my roommate a little longer. I'm going to see if there isn't a safer environment where I can release you. I'll try calling the zoo. Maybe they have a place for a little critter like you. You have so much personality; I know you would entertain the people if the zoo would just give you a chance. I'll call tomorrow, so you just relax until then, okay?" Lucky looked at me as if she understood me, gave a little chirp of what sounded like thanks, and disappeared into her house.

Chapter 6

NOT AGAIN!

Trying to find a safe place to release Lucky proved to be more difficult than I originally thought. The zoo turned out to be a bust; they didn't want her. According to the zoo personnel, she was a *nuisance*, and "squirrels are rodents, which means they are destructive and carry diseases." It didn't seem to matter to them that Lucky had been raised in captivity and had been to the vet. She just wasn't welcome there. Trying the Wildlife Rescue office again was no use either. There was still no answer from them, and they hadn't returned any of my phone calls. I couldn't help but wonder how much good they could be doing if they never returned anyone's phone calls. The forest ranger I called said that there was a new section of the forest that had recently opened to the general public. He suggested that maybe I could let her go there. The only problem with that area was that there was no civilization for miles, which meant the going would be rough. I would have to backpack into the forest for a long distance, carrying the squirrel and her cage over rough terrain. That *didn't* appeal to me if I could find another solution.

Lucky was beginning to feel the spring weather again, and, since she was now approximately seven months old, I decided to take her a little further up the mountain we lived on and release her again.

I found a spot I thought was excellent. The snows had begun to melt on this side of the mountain, so there were grassy areas where she could play, and there were trees close by for her to scamper up for protection. There was also no shortage of other squirrels for her to socialize with; so I once again released my little friend and watched her bound across the terrain, rushing up and down trees, exploring everything. I observed her for a little while and then knew I needed to get out of there so she didn't see me every time she looked back.

All the way home, I kept asking God to take care of His creation and protect her from harm and predators. My biggest concerns were the coyotes that were overrunning the area, and the cars that drove too fast up and down the roads that threaded their way through the forest region. But I had to have faith that this funny little creature would be alright, since there was nothing further I could do about it.

I slept poorly that night, worrying about Lucky, despite my earlier resolution not to, and awoke after only a few hours of sleep to a screeching outside. I lay in bed for a few minutes, trying to get my bearings. The sun had just come up, and I couldn't quite figure out what the racket was or exactly where it was coming from. Suddenly, it came to me! That sounded like Lucky's cry to me, and she sounded like she was in trouble. *Here we go again*, I thought.

Quickly getting dressed, I rushed outside calling Lucky's name. She answered me just as quickly, but I couldn't tell from which direction the sound was coming. So I kept calling and running in first one direction and then the other, trying to pinpoint where she was. I finally found her . . . under the hood of the pickup . . . her tail stuck in the fan belt! How she got it stuck, I had no idea. So I pulled the fan belt away from her tail, freeing her to go on her way. Once again, she ran up my arm to my shoulder.

"That's it, Lucky. I don't think you're ready to be on your own, yet. I think I need to keep you around awhile longer until you get a little older and can hopefully stay out of trouble!"

My first human treat!

Who's at the door

Chapter 7

LUCKY'S RELEASE

Lucky was almost a year old when I knew the time had finally come to release her into the wild. It was in the spring, and the days had gotten longer, with wildflowers blooming where just weeks earlier, snow had blanketed those same fields. Hummingbirds were zipping around, evidence of the end of a long, cold winter. And with the return of the hummers came a new population of squirrels, some young, some old, but all willing to scamper around, chasing each other up trees and over rock piles, chattering at each other as they played.

Lucky was moved out onto the screened porch, where she could observe the antics of others of her species. She seemed a little nervous when she first saw all the activity. In a few days, however, she was watching the other animals intently. Within about a week, she had moved herself up to the "penthouse suite" in her cage, where she could get a better view of everything going on outside the screened-in confines of the porch. If she could have gotten her nesting box up four levels, I'm sure she would have moved it. But instead, she pulled everything out of the box, making multiple trips to carry it all up to the top floor, and then she proceeded to make herself an "igloo" out of the contents. That way, she could crawl into it and pull a layer over herself when she wanted to retreat from the world.

A couple of weeks later, she was spending all her time observing the other squirrels. I had begun to withdraw, giving her attention only when I fed her or cleaned her cage. Even then, it was on a limited basis; I wanted her to get used to not having humans around. I wanted her "wild side" to show through and become the dominant part of her personality.

When I observed her mannerisms getting more aggressive and saw her grabbing onto the cage like a prisoner in a jail cell as she longingly watched the other squirrels, I called my friend to ask her if she would go with me to release Lucky. She was quite athletic, and I knew she could climb a tree to nail up Lucky's nesting box. I wanted Lucky to have something a little familiar so she could get used to being free a little at a time. I had no idea whether she would use it in the wild, but I felt confident she would use it at least the day we released her. My friend was also an animal lover and had been raised on a ranch, so she was used to having all kinds of animals around. She was thrilled to accompany me and knew it would be hard on me since I had gotten quite attached to this funny little creature.

That final morning with Lucky dawned bright and clear, with a slight nip in the air. I put off calling my friend as long as I could; I wanted to prolong the inevitable release of my little furry companion of the past year. But when I could drag my feet no longer—the sun was getting higher in the sky and I wanted Lucky to get used to her new environment before dark—I made the call. Heidi came over and helped me load Lucky's things into her pickup truck; we took food, water, treats, and all of her housing material. I transferred Lucky to her travel cage, stroking her wiry-haired little body one last time. This was going to be harder than I thought. I had really come to enjoy the little squirrel, despite the work she created for me. But I knew I had to do this, for her sake.

We drove Lucky to a slightly remote area in the national forest that would see babbling brooks from the spring runoff, wildflowers in bloom, and lots of other wildlife to teach her the ways of the wild. It also was an area that would not be too difficult to reach on foot while carting Lucky and her belongings. We each grabbed a load, and, equipped with hammer and nails and Lucky's travel cage, we set off.

It was rocky terrain, and the area where we wanted to put her house was down in a draw. We slowly made our way down the side of the canyon, with me holding Lucky's cage and Heidi bringing the nesting box

and a bag full of items we would need. We didn't have to hike a great distance, but because of the terrain, it took about thirty minutes to get to the tree we wanted for Lucky's new home. Heidi climbed the tree, with hammer and nail in her back pocket. I sat Lucky's cage on the ground and grabbed the nesting box. Putting some of her food and treats inside, along with all the nesting material she had gathered, I climbed as far as I could go holding the box in one hand and then stretched as far as I could to hand the box to Heidi. She reached down and, with the claw foot of the hammer, snagged the box, lifted it to her side, and grabbed it with the other hand. Wrapping an arm around a limb so as not to fall, she nailed Lucky's house to the tree. Heidi climbed down, and I tearfully opened Lucky's cage.

She had been watching our movements intently, and, as soon as I let her go, she scampered out, sniffed the base of the tree for only a few seconds, and then darted up the tree to her house. She poked her head in the opening, decided it was familiar enough, went in, and then stuck her head up through the hinged top and looked around. She was excited and started rearranging her "furnishings." Then, taking a break from her housecleaning, she scampered from limb to limb, running out as far on the branch as she could. She then paused, looked around at her surroundings, and bounded off to another limb and repeated the process. It was fun, and somehow comforting, to watch her. Finally, when little trickles of sweat coursed their way down my spine from standing in the sun, which had definitely warmed the day, I decided it was time to leave.

Picking up Lucky's travel cage and any evidence of our having been there, we left the area, looking back frequently. I knew it was the right thing to do, and I could see Lucky would be fine in her new environment, but I was truly going to miss my wiry-haired little friend. We drove off, and I said a little prayer that God would protect her, hoping nothing I had done over the past year would be a detriment to her well-being.

My new home away from home.

EPILOGUE

The days following Lucky's release found me outside, doing things around the property where I could constantly witness the multitudes of squirrels that were frolicking around the barn and running up trees, jumping from limb to limb. Others were hopping over each other on the ground and playing games that looked a lot like the game of tag that children play. I occasionally caught myself calling Lucky's name, the way I always called her, just to see if she would answer. But she never did. I was torn between wanting her to answer and knowing that if she did, I had failed at my release program, which would not have been good.

Then one day, about a year later, Heidi and I were having lunch, and we got to talking about Lucky. She animatedly told me that she had been riding her horse in that area recently and called Lucky, mimicking the sing-song voice I used to call her. She said, "I *know* Lucky is alright because there is one squirrel that answers back and runs to the end of the tree branch and just sits and looks at me, chirping like Lucky always did. That is the only squirrel around that does that, so it *must* be her. I really think Lucky Girl is fine." Now, I have no idea what a squirrel's lifespan is, or whether Lucky truly was out there on the trail Heidi took, but it has comforted me greatly to think that she is fine and living out her life among her own kind, finding a mate, and having little squirrels to scamper after and raise. I can only hope that maybe—because of my love of animals and my desire to help a tiny living creature beat the odds—my helping hand gave one of God's creatures a chance to live a full life, even if it was a life lived a bit unusually for a wild squirrel.

Looking back on those eventful eleven months, I realize that the little squirrel taught me a lot and took me on an adventure I will never forget. She taught me patience, above all. I had to exercise patience

every time I cleaned her cage, or fed her new foods, or replaced a chewed-through phone cord, or waited for her to finish her exercise routine of running up one of my arms and down the other. Yes, every step of the way required patience. She also taught me to have hope, and she renewed my faith. I prayed often that God would help this little creature that He had first put on this earth and then had caused me to come across in such a timely manner. I prayed that I would know the right thing to do with regard to her upkeep, because I had not found any information source that could tell me what I needed to know. I prayed about when to release her and that God would keep this funny little creature safe when I did let her go. And, I hoped that nothing I had done in the eleven months of raising her would be a hindrance to her in the wild.

Yet, I believe the best gift of all was the renewal of my sense of humor. I had just been diagnosed with Multiple Sclerosis and was having a hard time coping with the many things I could no longer do and with the outlook for the rest of my life. Depression was threatening my usually sunny disposition, and I wondered what my future held. Then, along came Lucky, who was a distraction from my thoughts and problems. I now had something else on which to focus my attention. She made me laugh so often, she probably thought, *This human is crazy!* But, she was definitely good for me. I can only thank God for Lucky's help through a difficult time in my life, and I hope and pray that I helped her in return.

I'm coming out the roof of my nesting box, but I blend in with the branches

The last view of my human
before she slips away.

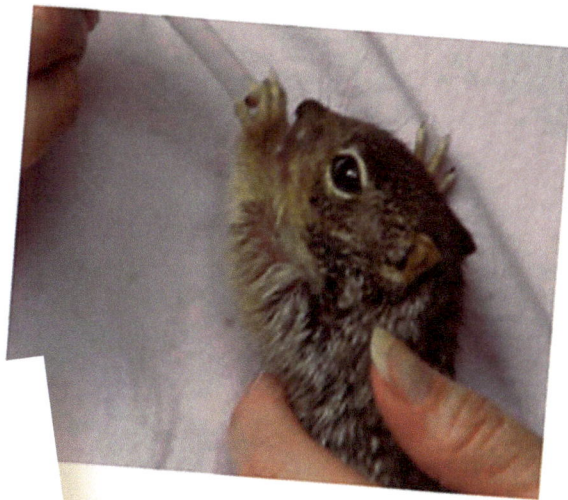

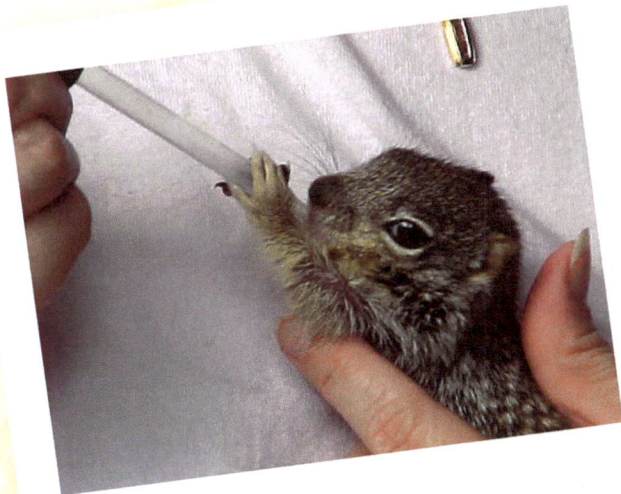

I love to run my sticky fingers
through your hair!

I didn't eat ALL the time.

CPSIA information can be obtained
at www.ICGtesting.com
Printed in the USA
BVHW020434171122
652114BV00002B/53